This book belongs to

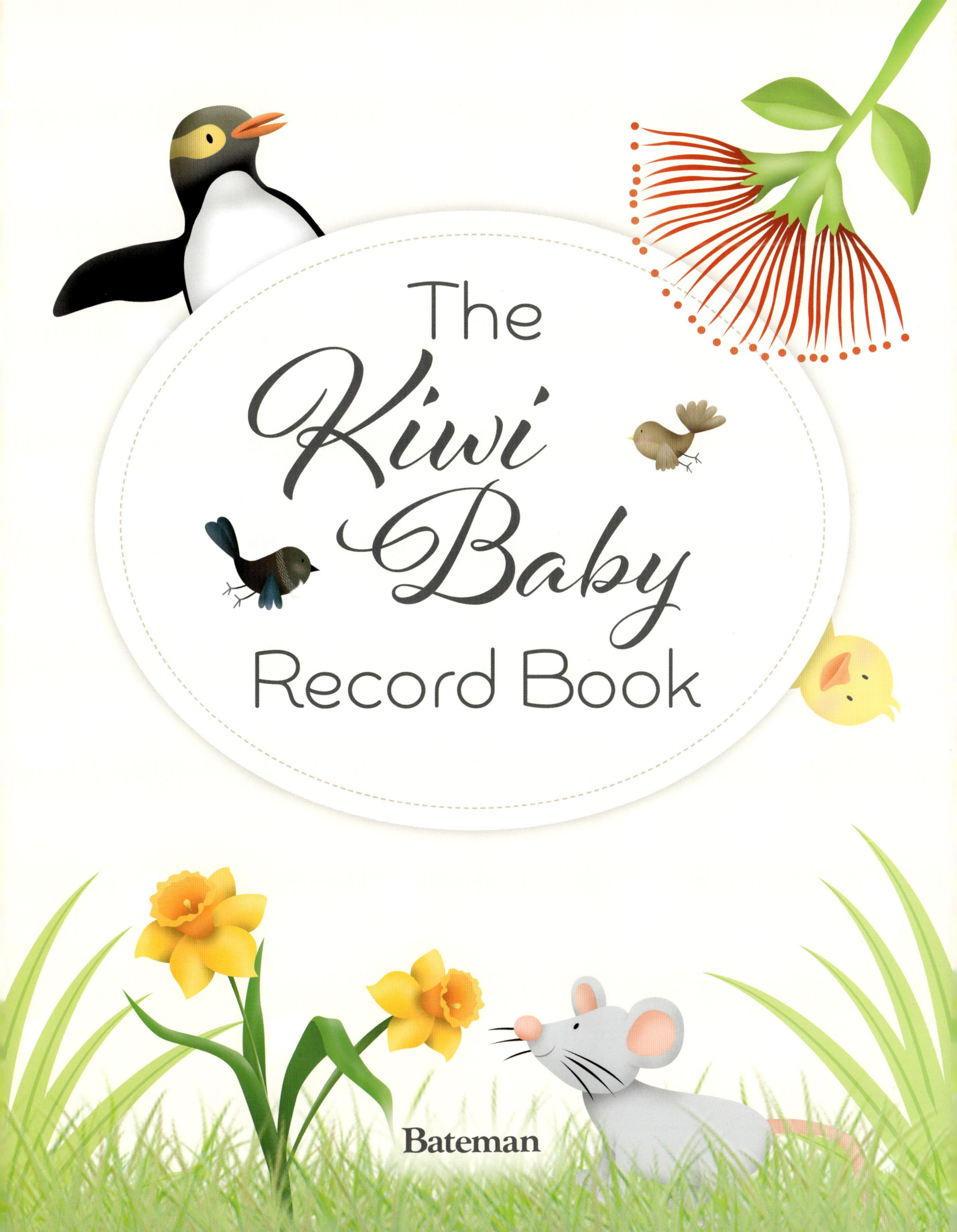
The
Kiwi
Baby
Record Book
Bateman

Compiled by Antoinette Sturny

Published in 2016 by David Bateman Ltd
Unit 2/5 Workspace Drive, Hobsonville, Auckland, New Zealand

Reprinted 2017, 2020, 2022

www.batemanbooks.co.nz

A catalogue record for this book is available from the National Library of New Zealand.

ISBN 978-1-86953-939-9

Publisher: Bill Honeybone
Illustrations and book design: Cheryl Smith, Macarn Design
Printed in China by Asia Pacific Offset Ltd

Contents

My Arrival

Date and time of birth

I was early / late / on time

Weight

Blood group

Length

Birthmarks

Circumference of head

Place of birth

Colour of eyes

Doctor's / Midwife's name

Colour of hair

Who do I look like?

My first photo

My first photo

Mementos

My hospital tags

My birth announcement

What Was Happening in the World?

First Days

My feeding times ______

Breast or bottle ______

Duration of each feed ______

Sleeping times ______

Preferred sleeping position ______

Wakeful times ______

Do I eat and sleep well? ______

Coming home date ______

Who was there to welcome me? ______

My first days photo
My first days photo

First Visitors

Visitors	Gifts

What My Family and Friends Said About Me

About Me

My full name is ______

My name was chosen by ______

because ______

I was christened / had a naming ceremony on ______

at ______

Comments ______

______

______

______

My star sign ______ My birth stone ______

My Chinese year ______ My birth flower ______

(see pages 42–43 for these)

My Room

My room photo

My Family Tree

Grandfather / Grandmother

Grandfather / Grandmother

Mother

Father

Brothers / Sisters / Me

Me and my family photo
Me and my family photo

My Early Milestones

I first held my head up

I first smiled

I first sucked my thumb / a dummy

I first discovered my hands

I first discovered my feet

I first recognised a voice

I first recognised my own name

I first made noises using my lips (*ba-ba, ma-ma, pa-pa*)

My first animal noise

My first word

I first said 'No!'

My early milestones photo
My early milestones photo

Eating

I first ate solid food ____________________

I was weaned from bottle / breast ____________________

I first drank from a cup by myself ____________________

My favourite finger food ____________________

I first fed myself ____________________

Food I like ____________________

____

____

Food I don't like ____________________

____

____

Me eating photo
Me eating photo

Getting Around

I first held my head up ______________________

I first sat up with help ______________________

I first sat up by myself ______________________

I first rolled onto my front ______________________

I first crawled ______________________

I first stood up by myself ______________________

I first took a few steps ______________________

I first start walking! ______________________

I first went on a car trip ______________________

I first went shopping in the pram ______________________

I first went on an outing in the stroller ______________________

Me getting around photo

Me getting around photo

My First Christmas

We spent Christmas at ____________________

Other people there ____________________

My favourite present ____________________

My first Christmas photo

First Holidays

We went to

from with

The weather was

My first paddle in the water

My first ice cream

My first holiday photo

My First Birthday

I live at ______________________________

My height is ______________________________

My weight is ______________________________

Things I say ______________________________

My favourite toys and books ______________________________

____

____

____

My Birthday Party

at ______________________________

with ______________________________

My presents ______________________________

My first birthday photo

My first birthday photo

My Favourite Things

Nursery rhymes ______________________________

Stories ______________________________

Music ______________________________

Clothes ______________________________

Animals ______________________________

DVDs / TV programmes ______________________________

Games ______________________________

Friends ______________________________

Food ______________________________

I don't like ______________________________

____

My favourite things photo
My favourite things photo

Bathtime

I first really enjoyed my bath ______

My first time in a big bath ______

My first bubble bath ______

My favourite bath toys ______

My first swim ______

My first time in the sea ______

My first play under the sprinkler ______

Me at bathtime photo

Me at bathtime photo

Bedtime

My sleep pattern as a newborn ______

My first unbroken night ______

My sleep pattern at six months ______

My favourite soft toy ______

My first time in a cot ______

My first time sleeping in a bed ______

My first babysitter ______

Me at bedtime photo
Me at bedtime photo

My Height

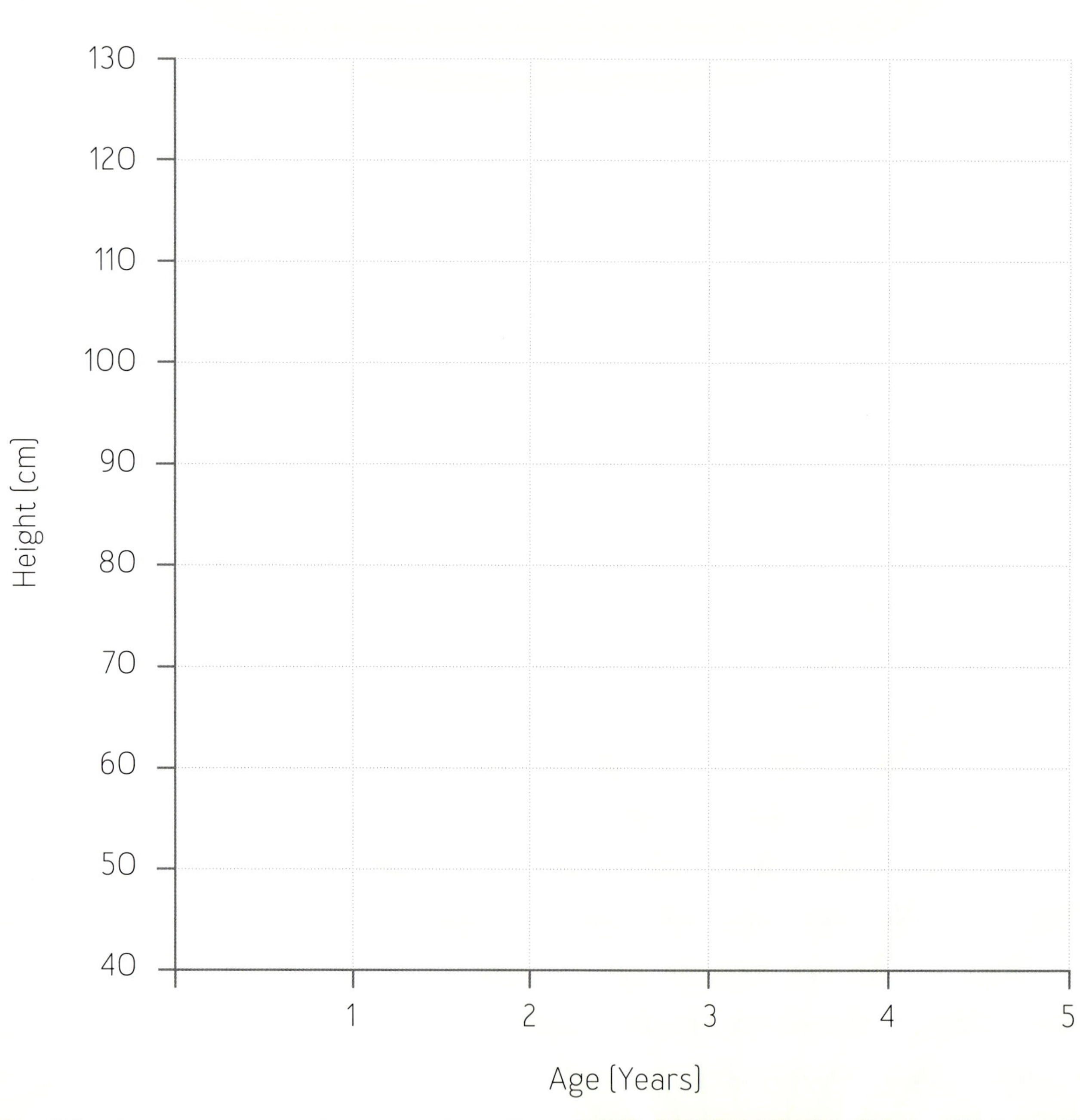

My Weight

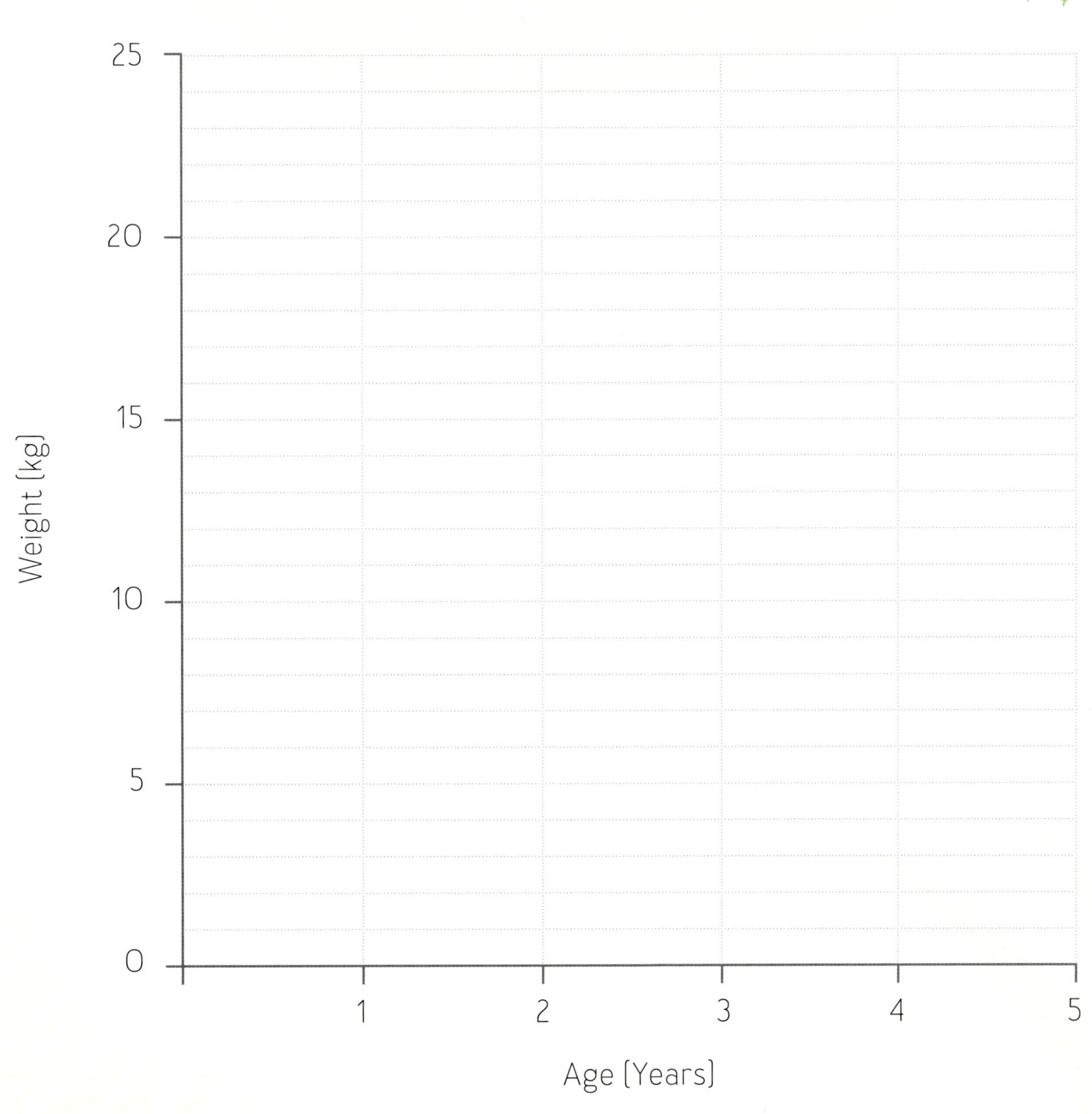

My Teeth

I got my first tooth on ____________________

I lost my first tooth on ____________________

I lost my second tooth on ____________________

I lost my third tooth on ____________________

I lost my fourth tooth on ____________________

The Tooth Fairy left me ____________________

Things to Remember

My handprint

My footprint

A lock of my hair

Medical Records

Vaccinations

Age	Vaccine	Date

Allergies ____________________

Common illnesses ____________________

____

Comments ____________________

____

Photos
Photos

The Future

What people say about me ______________________________

My personality ______________________________

Me showing my personality photo
Me showing my personality photo

What Am I Like?

Star signs

Aquarius
Jan 20th – Feb 18th

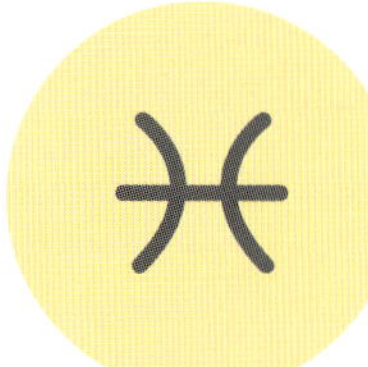

Pisces
Feb 19th – Mar 20th

Aries
Mar 21st – Apr 19th

Taurus
Apr 20th – May 20th

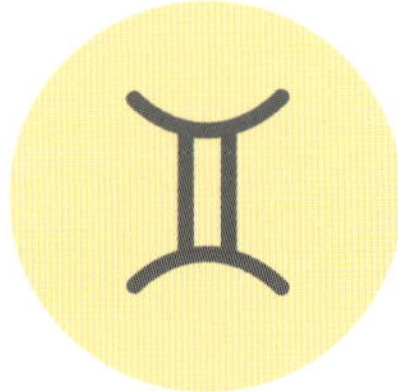

Gemini
May 21st – Jun 20th

Cancer
Jun 21st – Jul 22nd

Leo
Jul 23rd – Aug 22nd

Virgo
Aug 23rd – Sep 22nd

Libra
Sep 23rd – Oct 22nd

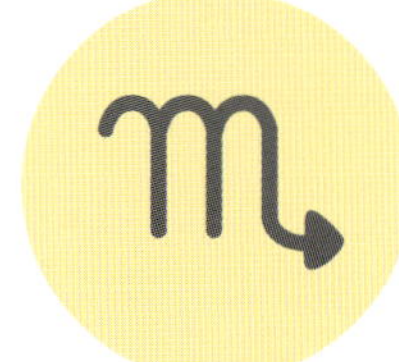

Scorpio
Oct 23rd – Nov 21st

Sagittarius
Nov 22nd – Dec 21st

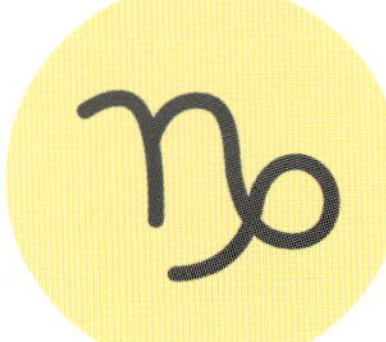

Capricorn
Dec 22nd – Jan 19th

Chinese Years

Rat	Ox	Tiger	Rabbit	Dragon	Snake	Horse	Goat	Monkey	Rooster	Dog	Pig
1960	1961	1962	1963	1964	1965	1966	1967	1968	1969	1970	1971
1972	1973	1974	1975	1976	1977	1978	1979	1980	1981	1982	1983
1984	1985	1986	1987	1988	1989	1990	1991	1992	1993	1994	1995
1996	1997	1998	1999	2000	2001	2002	2003	2004	2005	2006	2007
2008	2009	2010	2011	2012	2013	2014	2015	2016	2017	2018	2019
2020	2021	2022	2023	2024	2025	2026	2027	2028	2029	2030	2031

Birth stones and flowers

January	Garnet	Carnation
February	Amethyst	Primrose
March	Aquamarine	Daffodil
April	Diamond	Sweet Pea / Daisy
May	Emerald	Hawthorn / Lily of the Valley
June	Pearl	Rose/Honeysuckle
July	Ruby	Water Lily / Delphinium
August	Peridot	Poppy / Gladiolus
September	Sapphire	Morning Glory / Aster
October	Opal	Calendula / Cosmos
November	Citrine	Chrysanthemum
December	Blue topaz	Holly / Narcissus

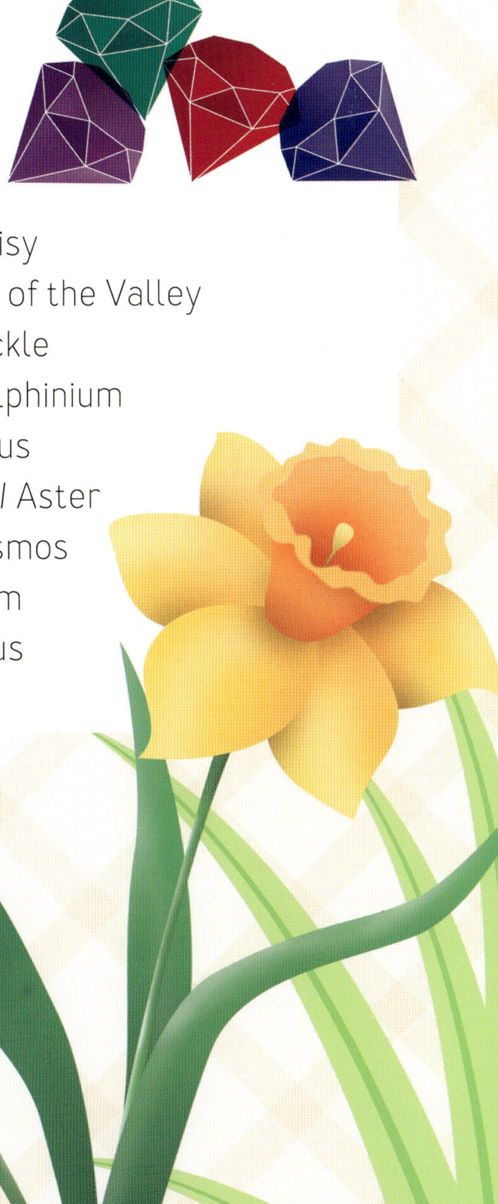

Photos